eBay 2019

Sell More Stuff

Table of Contents

Why eBay

Why should I sell on eBay when Amazon has more active users and doesn't charge any listing fees? I ask myself this question every day. And every day I struggle more and more to come up with a good answer.

eBay is a giant pain in the ass.

They constantly change the rules of the game in midstream. There seems to be no end to their service outages, mess ups, and programming errors. Every day, they make bad decisions that strangle small sellers and make it harder for them to establish a foothold on the site. eBay spent the last decade trying to convince everyone PayPal was the best payment method available, and now that they have spun PayPal off as a separate entity they are trying just as hard to undo all that.

And don't get me started talking about their fees. I could write an entire book bitching about how ridiculous and unfair they are, but who is going to listen, right?

I know, I sound like one of those crazy whiners and eBay haters who stalk the E-commerce Bytes Blog. Trust me, I'm not that guy.

When it comes down to it, I'm a raving eBay fan. I've been an eBay fanatic for the last twenty years. It's just that I'm not happy with the direction eBay has gone over the last five or six years. They may have a plan to turn things around. I hope they do, but if they have a plan it's not obvious.

In the end, the only good reason I can give you to sell on eBay is it works. I list my stuff on eBay and people send me money. When I list my stuff on Bonanza and eBid, it's like burying my stuff in a giant sinkhole because nothing sells.

That's what it's all about.

Now that I got that off my chest, let's talk about how you can rig the system, so you can make more money.

$5,000 a Month Selling on eBay and Amazon!

S ounds impossible, doesn't it? I'm here to tell you, I've done it—and, so have thousands of other sellers.

You can too!

It's just a matter of getting started.

I have new sellers ask me every day, "What's the secret to selling on eBay?" or "What's the best way to get started selling on Amazon?"

Here's what I tell, them, and what I'm going to tell you.

"Get started.

"List your first item today. Don't worry about what you don't know, or what you think you have to know.

"Just do it!"

. . .

It really is that simple.

I can tell you everything I know about selling on eBay. I can tell you what products to sell. I can tell you how much to charge, and what type of listing template to use. I can tell you the best time to start and end your listings, and how to ship your items, and on—and on.

But, there's one thing I can't do.

I can't make you get started.

Think about that for a moment. Every day hundreds of people buy guides just like this one. They read them from cover to cover. Many of them underline important passages, and scribble notes in the margins, or on a notepad.

They plan what they're going to do; what they're going to sell; and how much money they're going to make.

And, then...they begin to doubt themselves. They ask themselves questions—like what if it doesn't work? What if I list my items wrong? What if my items don't sell? What'll I tell my friends if I fail?

Does any of this sound familiar?

What I'm trying to help you understand here is simple.

We're all plagued by self-doubt. Everybody questions things when they're first getting started with something new. What you've got to do if you want to become successful is to overcome these doubts.

It's like learning to walk or ride a bicycle. Sometimes you're going to fall off.

When you do, you need to stand up, and put one foot in front of the other and keep moving. If you fall down, dust yourself off, and keep moving.

Selling online is similar to learning to walk.

You try one product or one listing. If your item doesn't sell, you find another one, and try again. If your item sells, you tweak your description or product, so you can sell even more.

If you don't learn anything else from reading this book, keep this one bit of information in the back of your mind.

Success is all about getting started.

Why you should sell on eBay

For the average person who wants to start an online business eBay and Amazon are the easiest ways to get started. Just list your items, and they will make them available to more than 400 million ready buyers. You don't have to do anything else. There's no SEO, no blogging, or costly PPC ads on Google or Facebook.

Just list your stuff on eBay or Amazon and you're in business.

. . .

If you're new to online selling—eBay and Amazon are a great way to cut your teeth in e-commerce.

Of the two sites, Amazon makes getting started the easiest. I like to compare it to hitching a ride on someone else's business. All you do is look for a listing similar to what you want to sell, and select the <sell on Amazon> button next to where it says "Have one to sell?" After that you follow the prompts—add your item condition, asking price, and presto, your item is for sale on Amazon.

It really is that simple.

Of course, not every item you run across is going to be available for sale on Amazon. Sometimes you stumble across a new or unique item no one has listed for sale yet. Not a problem. Amazon has a tool that lets you create a new listing page for it. We'll talk more about using it later in this guide.

Amazon also has a few restrictions on products you can sell, especially around Christmas and other big holidays. They don't want the little guys selling against them or their big merchants in these product lines. It's just one of those things you need to deal with. Most times when I bump into one of these categories Amazon shows me my listing has been blocked. Translation: it's not being shown to visitors on the Amazon website. It's still there, but only Amazon and I can see it.

. . .

eBay offers a similar feature. Under the pictures at top of the item listing page you'll see the words, "Have one to sell?" Next to that you'll see some blue text that says <Sell now>. Select that, and it will bring up an item description page pre-populated with many of the item details you need to list the item.

It's not quite as simple to use as Amazon's piggybacking feature, but with a few tweaks you can produce a great looking listing page. eBay requires you to add at least one picture of the product you are trying to sell. You can also change the description a bit to better fit the product you are selling. Maybe talk about the color, any accessories you are including, and add a little detail that describes any of the rough spots. Doing this helps potential buyers get a better feel for what you are selling.

And, just like Amazon, eBay lets you add new listing pages from scratch when you have an item unique to their website. We'll get more into that in another chapter. For now, keep in mind eBay and Amazon give you lots of flexibility in how you list and sell your items. The exact listing method you choose should be dictated by the item you are selling, the venue you choose to list it on, and what your individual sales goals are.

Which site should you sell on?

How do you decide which site is the best for what you are selling?

Generally speaking, eBay is better suited for selling unique, higher priced items, or items you are unsure about the value of. If you've got multiples of an item, eBay's auction feature allows you to experiment and test the waters. Auctions also give you a chance to get a higher price for items you are unsure of the value of, or items that have no set pricing. If you are nervous about not getting the price you want, you can set a reserve price. If your item doesn't hit the reserve price, it doesn't sell.

Use Amazon to list everyday items—books, textbooks, clothes, shoes, cell phones, and other electronics. Just about anything that is a consistent seller and sells within a set price range is perfect for selling on Amazon.

Amazon and eBay have a similar fee structure. Final value fees are slightly higher on Amazon, but they include payment processing fees. (On eBay, you make an extra payout for credit card processing.) Another great thing about Amazon is they don't charge listing fees. Amazon only gets paid if your item sells. Many writers have speculated eBay will switch to this strategy. Instead they keep raising their store listing fees. Go figure?

Amazon also makes it easier to determine how quickly your stuff should sell. Amazon ranks every item based on how well it sells. Take books as an example. There are millions of books listed for sale on Amazon. Each one has a product ranking from one to blah-blah million. The lower the ranking, the better the sales of the book are. Books ranked under 100 are super-fast sellers; books ranked under 10,000 are consistently good sellers; and books ranked under 50,000 still sell one or two copies per week.

Once you are familiar with Amazon's ranking system, it makes it easier to pick consistent winners.

Finding the best sellers on eBay takes a little more work. eBay's advanced search feature gives you a good idea how many of each item sold recently, and how much they sold for. By consistently using this information to source product you will sell more stuff at higher prices.

Start Selling on eBay

Almost every writer begins their eBay spiel by talking about what to sell or how to sell, but they are all missing the most important element to continued success selling on eBay. You need to build a strong reputation.

If you don't have awesome feedback, it's going to be tough to grow your sales.

If you are unfamiliar with buying and selling on eBay, buyers and sellers can rate each other based on a five-star rating system. The system is somewhat skewed towards buyers. If they are unhappy, they can leave negative feedback for the seller. Sellers can no longer leave negative feedback for buyers.

Buyers look at feedback to determine whether it's safe to purchase an item from a seller. If two sellers are offering the same item at a similar price, buyers will make their purchase from the seller who has better feedback. It just makes sense to spend your money with someone who has built a good reputation.

Your number one goal is to ensure customers are delighted with their purchases and leave you great feedback.

Sounds easy, doesn't it?

Let's look at some of the things that can go wrong.

- When customers make a purchase, eBay shows buyers an estimated delivery time. Top rated sellers generally ship their items within 24 hours, which means they are doing their part to ensure the item is delivered on time. Many times—the post office delivers packages outside of eBay's estimated delivery time. When this happens disgruntled buyers sometimes leave sellers negative feedback, even though the late delivery has nothing to do with them.

- Sometimes purchasers suffer from buyer's remorse. They change their mind before the seller ships the item. In eBay's early days, that wasn't a problem. The seller could send in a request to cancel the sale. When the buyer accepted it everything was okay. The reality today with eBay grading sellers on the defect system means when a buyer changes their mind they are really putting the seller on the spot. The seller is forced to choose between offering good customer service and canceling the sale or telling the customer "sorry—you're going to have to contact eBay to do that." The reason is when the buyer makes the request to cancel, the seller isn't charged with a defect. But, wait—there's a massive "Catch 22" lurking there. If the seller waits for the cancellation to go through eBay, the odds are he's going to be late with his agreed upon shipping time. That's a seller defect. Too many of them and you can be thrown off eBay.

- Here's another sticky situation sellers can find themselves in. Many times, customers make a purchase and then ask the seller to hold off on mailing the item until they return from vacation, or until it's closer to the recipient's birthday. Good customer service says you should listen to the customer, but if you do— eBay looks at it as a seller defect.

These are some of the situations you are going to face trying to offer good customer service while at the same time trying to maintain a low defect rate with eBay. I can't tell you how to deal with these issues. It's something you are going to have to work out on a case-by-case basis.

That's a quick overview of customer service.

. . .

Selling on eBay is all about creating great product listings that get customers excited about what you are selling.

How to Create A Great Listing

While there are no secrets to writing a great listing, I can give you a few tips that will make your listing pages more effective.

Great titles attract more buyers.

eBay gives you 80 characters to describe what you are selling. Make them count.

Here's a secret a lot of sellers don't know or understand. Your title contains the search terms for the stuff you are selling. It is how buyers find what you are selling amongst the millions of other things for sale on eBay.

Don't waste words.

Make every keyword count. The easiest way to do this is to think about how you would search for that item. What words would you use? What are the most important things you are looking for? Some of the obvious choices are—manufacturer, model number, color, condition—new, used, and refurbished, free shipping, and easy returns.

. . .

A Photo is Worth 1,000 Words.

Selling online is all about the pictures. Every day the internet is becoming more of a visual experience. Think about social media. The most shared items today are short videos, cat pictures, pictures of adults and children acting stupid, and those cutesy illustrations with quotes attached to them.

What does that mean for online sellers?

You need to include large clear pictures in all your listings. They need to show the item you are selling from several different angles. If the item has any damage, include close-up pictures of the affected areas.

Your pictures should be so clear your customer feels they can reach out and touch what you are selling. A cover designer on Fiverr explained this better than I ever could. She said the chocolate shown on her covers is so realistic you will want to lick it.

Make all your pictures that good, and you will find yourself making more sales for more money than ever before.

. . .

Sell the benefits, not the item.

Most sellers recite all these droll facts about what they are selling. "I have a yellow taxi cab from 1964. It has an AM radio, bald tires, a spare tire, and oh yeah—it only runs when you can get a few friends together to give it a push." Slightly humorous, but dull. It doesn't contain anything that compels you to buy the yellow taxi.

You need to create listings that mimic the way people read on the internet. Most people read the headlines, and then skim through the copy looking for details that interest them. If you list your key points using bullet points your customers eyes are going to move directly from the headlines to the bullet points.

Another mistake sellers make is rambling off a slew of features. Customers don't care about features. They want to know what's in it for them. Tell them the benefits.

- Your new TV comes equipped with a full featured remote, so you never have to get out of your chair to change the channel or adjust the volume.

- Your new theater chairs are awesome. They have a built-in refrigerator and urination control system, so you never miss a moment of programming to grab another beer or go number one.

. . .

Price your stuff to sell.

Inexperienced sellers rush to post their listings for sale, then settle for whatever price they get. Successful online sellers research every item before they post their listing. That way they know how likely it is to sell, how much money they can reasonably expect to get for it, and what the best keywords are to include in their title and listing description.

The more time and research you put into selling an item the more money you are going to make.

. . .

Write a Compelling description.

This means you need to describe your item—warts and all.

Making a successful sale online or in person is all about managing buyer expectations. Your listing needs to get buyers excited about what you are selling. You need to make them visualize your item, and picture how much fun they are going to have using it. But, before you go in for the kill, you need to make them pull back for a moment. List any defects or blemishes your item has. If you are selling a cell phone, be sure to tell potential buyers which carriers it is and is not compatible with.

Many sellers are afraid to mention problems or defects, because they think it will kill the sale. A lot of times it does just the opposite. When you take time out to explain defects and any potential problems they may encounter buyers are more likely to feel they can trust you.

Start Selling on Amazon

N o matter what anyone tells you, you need to sell on more than one platform. My advice would be to start on eBay and spread out to Amazon as quickly as you can.

Selling on Amazon is easier than selling on eBay.

To list an item for sale on Amazon just search for an item similar to the one you want to sell. Look the listing over to make sure it's the proper edition, variation, size, or whatever. When you are sure it's the correct item, look for the text that says, "Have one to sell." Select the box next to it that says <Sell on Amazon>.

When you select <Sell on Amazon> it pulls up the listing page. Verify that it's the correct item. Select the appropriate condition and make any condition notes in the box. Below that list the quantity available and your asking price. After you input the quantity you have available to sell, you can upload up to six images. The final step is to select your shipping preferences. You can select one shipping method, or all of them. One thing

I've discovered is most buyers go with the least expensive shipping option, but your item will sell quicker if you offer more options. Try it for yourself and see what happens.

Select continue and you will be taken to a summary page that reviews your selections and recaps your asking price and the expected Amazon fees if your item sells. It also tells you how much money you will receive after Amazon fees, and how much your shipping credit is.

If you have multiple items to sell, don't just list them together at the same price. Carefully examine their condition. If one item is in better condition, list it separately. Normally you can charge a higher price for an item in better condition.

A close look at the book category shows prices ranging from 99¢ to $25.00 or more depending on each book's condition. That's why it is so important to grade your book properly. In poor to good condition it may sell for 99¢, but the next step up can increase the selling price by $3.00 to $5.00.

Best advice. Grade your book as high as the condition warrants, but don't bump the grade just to make a few extra bucks. Grading items incorrectly is a sure way to get returns, or negative feedback.

. . .

Unless you sell one-of-a-kind collectibles, the listing method shown above is going to work for most of the items you list on Amazon.

When you have a unique item to sell that hasn't previously been listed on Amazon you can add a new page to the Amazon catalog. It takes a few more steps but will be a breeze after you have completed a few.

Follow these steps to add a new listing page to the Amazon catalog.

1. In Amazon Seller Central go to the inventory page and select <Add a Product>.
2. Enter the name of the product you want to list, the ISBN, or UPC.
3. Select a category to list your item in.
4. From here you will be taken to the listing page. Most listing pages have six separate sections.

- **Vital info** lets you enter the title for your item. Amazon allows you to add up to 250 characters. These are the search terms for your listing so make your keywords count. The other information you are asked for depends upon the item you are selling. Fill in as much information as possible.

- **Offer** lets you add a SKU (an identification number for the product. If you don't enter one, Amazon will select one for you.) This is also where you enter price, and the number of items you have for sale. Select the condition, add a condition note if needed, and select your shipping methods.

- **Images** is where you enter your product photos. Amazon requires photos to be 1000 pixels on the longest edge, and 500 pixels along the shortest edge. You are allowed up to eight pictures. Use as many as you need to sell your item.

- **Product description** gives you 2000 characters to describe your item. Keep it short and simple. List any accessories included with your item. If there is damage—describe it. Unlike eBay—Amazon does not allow you to list any branding information about yourself or your business, so keep your description focused on the products you are selling.

- **Keywords** lets you add keywords and search terms to make it easier for buyers to find what you are selling. Each section has four spaces that accept up to 50 characters.

- **More details** lets you include item and package dimensions.

After you have completed all six sections, select <save and finish> at the bottom, and your item should be listed on Amazon within fifteen to thirty minutes.

The above categories will vary based upon what you are selling. The example I used was from the book's category.

Changes for 2018 / 2019

As usual, eBay is in a state of constant flux. Fees are going up, payment methods are undergoing a major shift, and the refund policy is evolving.

Seller fees

eBay's says they "keep the fees simple, so you can focus on your business." That may or may not be true. I will leave the answer up to you.

For casual sellers, nothing has changed. They get 50 free listings every month. After that, they pay 35 cents for each additional listing, more in certain categories. Final value fees run another 3.5 percent to 12 percent in most categories.

If you sell books, DVDs, or CDs the final value fee jumped from 9.15 percent to 12 percent in September 2018.

eBay Stores

eBay used to offer three different store levels. Now they have five, with a cost that runs between $4.95 to $2999.95 per month. All of them come with an allotment of free and discounted listings.

Most sellers will go with one of the first three levels.

A Starter store runs $7.95 per month, less with a yearly subscription. It includes one hundred free fixed price listings and one hundred free auction listings. Additional listings are 30 cents in either category.

A Basic store starts at $27.95 per month, less with a yearly subscription. It includes 250 fixed price and 250 auction listings. Additional listings are 25 cents each in either category.

A Premium store begins at $74.95 per month, less with a yearly subscription. It includes 1,000 free fixed price listings and 500 free auction listings. Additional auction listings cost 15 cents, fixed price listings cost 10 cents.

Anchor stores took a major jump in price. The cost is $349.95, less with a yearly subscription. It includes 10,000 fixed price listings and 1,000 auction listings. Additional auction listings cost 10 cents, fixed price listings cost 5 cents.

Enterprise stores are for the big boys. They start at $2999.95 and offer no yearly discounts. A subscription includes 100,000 fixed price listings and 2,500 auction listings. Additional auction listings cost 10 cents, fixed price listings cost 5 cents. Larger packs are available that include 10,000 or 50,000 additional fixed price listings. Expect to pay up for the privilege.

eBay also has a punishment fee for sellers that don't meet their minimum standards. They tack an extra four percent onto the final value fees.

Managed Payments

The other big change for sellers going forward is Managed Payments on eBay. For most sellers it sounds like a good thing. Instead of making their payment through PayPal, buyers will make their payments on eBay.

For sellers, Managed Payments mean no more waiting to get your money. eBay will deposit all money received into your account daily. That means you can cut up your PayPal debit card and start using your debit card. If everything goes well the move should improve seller cash flow.

Managed Payments is going to take time.

eBay began rolling the program out in September 2018 and figures it will be 2021 before all sellers are enrolled in the program.

For buyers used to making payments through PayPal, eBay Managed Payments may seem a little weird at first. It's the same process they are using on Amazon and other e-commerce websites, so buyers should adjust easily enough.

Refunds are more problematic

In the past, sellers were able to decide whether they would accept returns or not. Not anymore. eBay offers a site wide Money Back Guarantee on most items.

eBay's Money Back Guarantee protects buyers in case they don't receive their item, or it arrives not as described in the listing. It covers buyers for "up to 30 days after you received your item (or when you should have received it)." After that, PayPal extends protection for 180 days.

What's a seller to do? Whether your store policy says you accept refunds or not, eBay and PayPal policy override your settings.

When a buyer opens a case against you, take it seriously. You have three days to resolve the buyer's issue. If you can't come to a resolution, eBay will step in and issue a decision within 48 hours.

The odds are you aren't going to like eBay's decision, so work with your buyer. Do what it takes to make them happy. Give your buyer a refund even if it doesn't make sense for you. Offering a full refund may prevent your receiving negative feedback.

The alternative isn't good.

eBay is up front on their policy page and tells sellers, "in most cases, if you issue a full refund to the buyer before we're asked to step in, we'll credit your final value fees." If you don't, it's left unsaid, but the understanding is they will refund the full payment and keep your final value fees.

You might as well just man up and refund the payment. Chalk it up as an additional cost of doing business.

12 Tips to Grow Your Business

H ere are twelve tips that will help you grow your business and make more money in 2019. Use one or use all of them. They have helped me build a more successful online business.

. . .

Offer amazing customer service

Customer service is the most important element of selling on eBay.

Customer service begins with a great listing. Provide large clear photos of every item you sell. If the item you are selling has any damage or blemishes, take close-up pictures of those areas. Give customers the information they need then let them decide if the item is right for them or not.

The same thing goes for your description.

Make your product descriptions short, easy to read, and benefit focused. Get right to the point. Identify the product, model number, maker, and any other relevant information. If it's new in the box, or new without tags, tell your buyer exactly what they are getting. If the item is damaged in any way, describe the damage, and refer the customer to your photos so they can make their own decision.

Finally, list the benefits buyers will enjoy when they purchase your item.

- This digital camera comes with a backup battery, so you can take pictures to your heart's content and never worry about running out of power.

- This heavy-duty rubber case protects your iPhone whether you drop it from 1 inch or 10 feet. Stop worrying and start enjoying your new iPhone.

Do you understand the difference?

No one wants an extra battery. They want the satisfaction they get from not having to worry about their battery going dead. No one wants a heavy-duty rubber iPhone case. They want to know their phone is protected from accidental damage.

When you focus on the benefits customers will receive from buying your item, you make them scream out, "Yeah! I have to have that."

And, that brings us to the final point. Keep your description short. Use plenty of white space, headlines, and bullet points.

Make it easy for buyers to find the information they are looking for.

Follow up with buyers.

When a potential buyer sends a request asking for more information, answer the email promptly. Use the eBay app so you know when someone asks a question while you are at work or on the go. If you can't answer the specific question right away, tell the customer you are away from your office, but will get back to them as soon as possible. Then give them a time frame and follow up within that period.

When you answer a customer inquiry there are all sorts of ways to approach it. Thank the customer for contacting you. Give them a little information about the item and your business. Then answer the specific question.

If a customer contacts you about an iPad you are selling and is concerned about a scratch on the screen shown in one of your pictures, here's how to respond to that customer.

"Thank you for visiting Braun's Apple-o-rama. We do our best to offer top quality used and refurbished Apple products at the best possible prices. One way we do that is by accurately describing every product we sell and providing clear accurate photos of the item you are buying. To answer your question, I just looked at the iPad you inquired about. It is in real nice shape, and comes with a case, and charger. The scratch you are asking about is roughly ½ inch long and runs along the surface. It does not go deep into the screen. I tested it out using Word and the internet and am happy to report the scratch does not affect viewing at all. I hope that answers all of your questions, and keep in mind we offer a 14-day 100% satisfaction guarantee—so if you are unhappy for any reason, feel free to return the item."

What do you think?

It's friendly. It tells a little more about your business, and how you approach selling online. It answers the customer's specific question, and it goes a step further to sell the item by stressing the 14-day money back guarantee.

Try using this approach in your business emails. Your customers are going to love it.

. . .

Use eBay / Amazon Shipping tools.

Many sellers still waste time hand addressing their packages and taking them to the post office.

eBay and Amazon have built in tools that make it easier to ship the stuff you sell and save you time and money. By using online shipping tools, you also help to ensure your customers receive their items quicker.

Here are some of the ways using these tools can help you ship more efficiently.

- eBay and Amazon shipping tools automatically transfer the customer information to your shipping label. You don't have to worry about addressing mistakes.

- The shipping tools verify addresses against postal records to ensure you are shipping to a valid address. If it turns out the customer provided a bad address, you can correct it before shipping your item. That saves you the cost of reshipping an item, and by verifying the address is correct, it helps your customer get their package quicker.

- When you use eBay and Amazon shipping tools you receive a discount over rates you would receive from going to the post office. In most cases tracking is free when you print your shipping labels online. That saves you a minimum of $1.05 for each item you ship.

- You can order packing supplies needed to ship items by priority and express mail, and you can schedule a home pick up, so the post office comes to you, rather than waste your time taking packages to them.

More advanced sellers, or sellers who transact business on more than one ecommerce platform, may want to check out Stamps.com or Endicia. They collect all your orders from the different platforms and let you ship from one console.

. . .

Research everything.

You never know. That item you bought for a dollar might be worth $500, or $5,000. Before you start it at 99¢ do a little research first, so you know what you've got.

On Amazon, you can tell how well an item is selling by looking at its product rank. In most cases Amazon gives a rank from 1 (being the bestselling item) to blah-blah million (being the slowest seller in that category). When you are sourcing products to sell, you want to pick items that rank under 100,000 whenever possible. This means that in most categories the products are still selling one or two items per week. If the item you want to sell ranks over 100,000 in its category, you might have to wait months or years for it to sell.

Some sellers hit book sales and clearance aisles at Wal-Mart, Target, and T J Maxx with scanners and scouting software to help select the items most likely to sell fastest for the best profit. If this sounds like something that might be of interest to you check out **Barcode Booty** by Steve Weber. It covers the topic of using scanning software in more detail.

If you are a weekend warrior, download the Amazon or eBay app to your smartphone. Check what some of the items you are considering purchasing sell for on eBay. That item you expected to make a killing on might be a real dog.

If you are selling on eBay, there are numerous research tools available from eBay and from third party sellers. The most useful tool for sellers is eBay's advanced search tab. It lets you see how many items have recently sold, how much they sold for, the listing method used for making the sale, and the starting price and or buy-it-now price.

My advice is to conduct basic research before listing any item. You can use the information to set a price and help select keywords and description ideas.

To access the advanced search tool, scroll up to the top of the eBay page where you see the search bar. Next to it you will see the word **advanced**. Select it, and you are ready to roll.

. . .

Offer refunds.

No one likes to take things back. You are on eBay to make money, not give it back.

A generous refund policy will help you sell more stuff. Buying online is scary. No matter how many items you have bought on eBay or Amazon, you always have lingering doubts. Did the seller accurately describe his item? Is that new iPhone he is selling new in the box? or is it a refurbished model being passed off as new?

Go ahead. Admit it. You've had those same doubts when you were getting ready to make an online purchase.

Take it from someone who's offered a 100 per cent satisfaction policy for the past ten years. Offering to give a refund doesn't mean customers are going to take advantage of you.

People are basically honest.

If you accurately describe what you are selling, and grade your stuff honestly, customers are going to be pleased with their purchases. Most refunds happen because of misunderstandings.

Your job as a seller is to help set buyer expectations so they understand what they are buying. You do this by describing any damage or problems, and by posting large clear photographs.

. . .

Take great photos.

The old saying is, "A picture is worth a thousand words." On eBay and Amazon, a picture can easily be worth a thousand dollars.

Throughout this book I've talked about the importance of taking great pictures. Pictures are the key to making more sales on eBay and Amazon. When buyers shop at a retail store they can pick items up, look them over, touch them, turn them over, and get a real feel for what they are buying. If you want to make more sales online, your pictures have to give customers that same shopping experience.

How do you do it?

The first thing you need is a good camera. The eBay app lets you post listings from your iPhone or smartphone. That's fine for occasional sellers. If you are a professional seller, that's not going to cut it. Cell phone pictures often come out grainy. Because of that they are hard to edit.

A good digital camera with a variety of lenses will let you take the best possible pictures. Most of the new cameras make it as easy as 1 – 2 – 3. You just point, the camera, press the button, and you get a great picture.

If you are photographing a lot of small items, consider purchasing a light box. You can pick one up on eBay or Amazon starting at $30.00. A light box normally comes with several floodlights, a tent-like structure to photograph your item in, a small tripod, and several different colored backdrops. The biggest advantage of using a light box is you can take close up photos of smaller items without worrying about dark backgrounds or weird looking shadows in your pictures.

If you are selling bigger items—furniture, bikes, exercise equipment, cars, etc. photograph them outside. It will give you the best possible lighting.

Best advice. Look every item you are selling over before you photograph it. If there's any kind of damage make sure you take pictures of the damage from several different angles.

Next think about what you are selling. What do customers need to see to purchase the item? How many different angles do you need to photograph it from? Are there working parts that customers would want to see? If you are selling a laptop or phone, would it make sense to show it lit up and working? How about accessories? If it comes with a power cord, CDs, ear buds, or a case, you should probably have a grouped photo of them.

Use as many pictures as you need to tell your story. Keep in mind eBay requires your picture to be at least 500 pixels along the longest edge. They recommend 1600 pixels for optimal viewing when your picture is enlarged. Amazon requires pictures to be at least 1000 pixels along the largest end, and at least 500 pixels along the shortest end.

. . .

Develop a pricing strategy.

Sellers have all sorts of pricing strategies. Some like to go for the highest price possible. Others start everything at 99¢ and are happy with whatever they get. Still others shoot for the middle ground, thinking they don't need to get the highest price possible, but they would still like a decent return on their investment.

Best advice. Determine a pricing strategy before you start selling online. Understand up front that it's okay to be the high price seller or the low-price seller, so long as you know why you are at that price point.

If you sell cheap crap, or rush to list a hundred items a day without putting any thought or time into them, the best you can hope for is to get the low price. If, on the other hand, you take time out to carefully research each item, shoot amazing photographs, and write an awesome benefit driven description, you have every right to ask for—and receive a higher price.

The price your item sells for is ultimately up to you.

What I suggest is to look at different items being sold on eBay and the different prices sellers are asking for them. You will find a lot of books, clothes, whatever people are asking a crazy amount of money for. But, you will also see a lot of sellers who pop the same item up for sale starting at 99¢ or $9.99. The low-end sellers generally have a single blurry picture, a short blah-blah description, and mixed or negative feedback. High end sellers include six to twelve well-lit photos in each listing and use the description to build value into the item and sell it for all it's worth.

The choice is entirely up to you. You can nickel and dime your way to mediocre success, or you can sell fewer items and make more money.

The profit you make on eBay is all about how you approach your listings.

Amazon is an entirely different animal when it comes to pricing. Because most items are sold off the same listing page, you need to stick to a lower price to stay in the ball game. The trick to making more sales on Amazon is to grade your items properly so you can sell your item as a higher-grade article.

Another secret to making money on Amazon is to steer away from the pack. Create your own items to sell.

It's not hard. Bundle a collection of James Patterson books together. Instead of listing each book for sale at 99¢ individually, price your bundle at $25.00. Create Halloween or birthday party packs centered around a theme. Include piñatas, plates, napkins, party favors and bags. If you sell electronic parts or kits include a short video or booklet that explains how to use them or hook them up. Now you are selling a complete solution rather than just a cord or a pile of parts. It makes it different enough from what other sellers are offering, so you can create your own listing page and ask for more money.

The trick is to make your item unique. That way you can create your own sales page on Amazon. When you do this competition and price are no longer a factor. You can create an amazing description and ask for—and receive a premium price.

Whenever possible, ask yourself how you can stack the deck in your favor. It will pay off every time.

. . .

Choose a niche to sell in.

Anybody can sell a little bit of everything on eBay. Most Top-Rated-Sellers learned early on they can make more sales and charge higher prices by specializing in a niche.

Brick and mortar stores rely on repeat customers to grow their business. Online sellers are no different. Repeat customers are going to be the lifeblood of your online business.

If you are selling clothes this week, books the next week, and bathroom accessories the week after it's going to be tough to build a repeat clientele. If you specialize in one product line, you are more likely to attract repeat buyers. If someone buys something from you that they like or collect, and they see you regularly sell similar items, they are more likely to check back to see what's next. Curiosity is your best friend. It will bring many buyers back to see what you are offering next week, and the week after.

So long as you don't disappoint customers and continue to offer new and unique items in your niche, they will keep coming back for more.

The question you are probably asking yourself is, "How do I let buyers know that I offer similar items?" Both eBay and Amazon offer online stores to their sellers. Make sure you set them up and keep them stocked with new and exciting items.

It's easier to brand yourself on eBay.

Each eBay listing invites buyers to visit your eBay store, or to view your other listings. Because Amazon is a marketplace made up of many sellers for each individual item, buyers don't get that nudge to look at individual listings from a single buyer. They can visit your Amazon storefront, but to do so, they need to know how to navigate there. Most buyers don't.

Let's talk about branding on eBay for a few more moments.

eBay offers sellers numerous opportunities to brand yourself. The most obvious one is to open an eBay store. You can design a custom storefront and listing template that makes shopping with you unique. You can include your logo, tag line, and any other info you care to include about yourself or your business. The downside is doing this is expensive and using HTML code in your listings has been found to hurt sales coming from mobile devices.

An easier and less expensive way to encourage repeat buyers is to talk about your other items in each of your listings. Remind buyers to check back regularly because you have a fluid inventory that is constantly changing, and you have new items arriving every week. If you have made a special-purchase you will be listing in upcoming weeks talk it up in all your listings. If you sell winter coats, mention visitors should check your eBay store for a great selection of gloves, scarfs, and hats. If you sell digital cameras, tell buyers to visit your store for batteries, bags, books, and lenses.

Make it fun. Make it educational.

Motivate your buyers to come back and check you out week after week. It will build repeat buyers and encourage customers to recommend you to their friends.

. . .

Sell international.

Most new sellers avoid international sales like the plague. Many of them have heard horror stories about items lost or stolen in transit, areas that form a Bermuda Triangle like zone that suck up eBay packages, and dishonest buyers who will take you for whatever they can get.

The actual truth about international selling is quite different than most people's perception of it. Most international sales go smoothly with many customers in Europe receiving their packages quicker than buyers here in the United States.

Several years ago, eBay instituted something called the Global Shipping Program that makes selling internationally no different than selling domestically.

The way it works is sellers opt into the Global Shipping Program when they list their item for sale. If their item sells to an international buyer, eBay provides the seller with the address of one of their shipping partners. You ship the item to eBay's U S shipping center, and your part in the transaction is completed. From that point on, eBay and Pitney Bowes are responsible for the safe delivery of your package.

It doesn't get much simpler than that.

And, in case you are still not convinced selling internationally is in your best interest, consider this— Most of the growth eBay sellers are experiencing is a direct result of international sales. Many successful sellers on eBay and Amazon draw as much as forty to fifty percent of their sales from international customers.

If you choose only one method to grow your sales, sell international.

. . .

Open an eBay store.

If you are serious about selling on eBay, open an eBay store. Over time, it's going to save you money. These days, eBay stores come with a variety of useful features—free and discounted product listings, discounting tools, extra pages to provide additional product information, and email list building tools.

Think of an eBay store as your own little space on the internet. Back in prehistoric eBay times (the early 2000's), most items sold at auction. On a good week 40 to 50 percent of the items you listed sold. If you relisted them two or three times a few more would sell.

The mathematicians among you have probably already figured out that that still leaves roughly 40 percent of your listings unsold. That begs the question, what's a seller to do with the rest of your items? One choice was to delete them, and figure they had their day. No one wanted them. Another choice was to pack them away in an eBay store and wait for buyers to stumble across them. In those dark days eBay didn't display store listings in search. Potential buyers had to do some extra work to ferret them out.

I took the last option and built an eBay store. I packed nearly 10,000 items away in my eBay store. The funny thing was—over time, I was selling more items from my eBay store than I was from my auction listings. If I took a week or two off from listing items, I could still make $500 or a $1000 a week.

That's the real beauty of an eBay store. I liken it to building an annuity. Not listing items for sale one week or listing a slew of bad items now and then won't kill your business. Your eBay store will help level out your sales and your income.

An eBay store comes with numerous seller tools that can help you ratchet up your sales.

- Promotions Manager (formerly Markdown Manager) lets you run spot sales. You can choose how long you want your sale to run, the percentage discount or dollar discount you want to offer, and which items you want to include in the sale.

- Mail list manager lets you build a mailing list of customers who sign up to receive mailings from you. Each time you create a sale with Promotion Manager you can choose to have eBay send an email to your customer list.

- Custom pages allow you to create additional pages to provide more information to your potential customers. Some sellers use them to provide sizing information for clothing, other sellers use them to talk about the products they sell, or how carefully they package and ship items. How you use your custom pages is entirely up to you.

- Promotional boxes let you collect and receive information from your customers. I use mine to explain my shipping policies and prices, ask customers to sign up for my mailing list, and I have one in the sidebar to my store that introduces new customers to my business and the products I sell.

- Custom categories let you set up sections within your eBay store that make it easier for customers to find items they are searching for.

. . .

Build an email marketing list.

Things change. Selling on eBay and Amazon may be the greatest thing going today, and you may be making all the money you want. But, tomorrow is another day.

You never know what's around the corner. There are a lot of former eBay power sellers who woke up one morning and discovered their entire $100,000 a year eBay business turned upside down.

Think it can't happen to you?

Five years ago, digital download products (eBooks) were some of the hottest sellers on eBay. Many sellers were cashing in selling hundreds of them per day. A lot of other sellers purchased them just to get quick feedback. And, then one day, eBay announced they were banning the sale of digital downloads. The new rules prohibited digital downloads and required that all eBooks had to be physically shipped to buyers on a CD or some other media.

Thousands of power sellers saw their businesses destroyed overnight.

More recently, eBay upgraded seller standards and changed the way they grade seller performance. Five-star feedback isn't good enough anymore. Sellers are evaluated based upon their defect rate. One and two-star ratings count as defects. So, does cancelling orders because you ran out of stock or any other reason. If your defect rate is over five percent, eBay reserves the right to limit or suspend your selling privileges. They reach back from three to twelve months to determine if you are compliant. To date thousands of five-star sellers have been booted off eBay for no other reason than eBay changed the way they evaluate your performance.

Amazon has been known to make similar changes. At certain times of the year, especially around Christmas only preapproved sellers can sell in certain categories. Other categories are limited to favored sellers year around. Most recently Amazon decided only a select group of sellers would be allowed to sell DVDs with an MSRP over $25.00. Many DVD retailers found themselves stuck with unsellable inventory, while at the same time having their ability to make a living limited.

That's why I say, no matter how well your online business is doing today—start building a mailing list to protect and grow your business.

. . .

The first thing you need to know is when you make a sale on eBay and Amazon—according to both company's TOS those customers belong to eBay and Amazon—not you, so you need to be careful how you contact them.

eBay lets you build an email list using their tools, but the email list belongs to them, and all emails must be sent through their email service.

The best way for sellers to build their email list on eBay is to include a promotional box on your eBay store page that asks sellers to join your email list. You can also suggest in your listings that sellers join your email list, so they know about upcoming sales and special events. When you do this, each time you create a sale using Markdown Manager you can send an announcement to your customer list.

Building a mailing list off eBay requires a little more effort and subterfuge.

Be sure to include a thank-you note in each package you send. Let customers know if they have any problems or questions you will be happy to help them out. If you have a website, list your URL and suggest customers visit it often as you are constantly adding new items to your inventory.

Suggest customers join your mailing list. Offer them free gifts or special discounts for doing so.

When you invite customers to join your list you are going to need an email service to sign them up. Some of the more popular email services are Mail Chimp, Constant Contact, and A Weber. The reason you don't want to do it yourself is there are privacy laws in place concerning email contact and sending spam emails. These services allow customers to easily opt into and out of your email program, thus ensuring you stay compliance with government regulations.

Detailed instructions about building an email list are beyond the scope of this book. Here are a few sources you may find helpful if you decide to setup an email list for your online business.

- **Email Marketing Blueprint** by Steve Scott
- **Email Marketing That Doesn't Suck** by Michael Clark, Stever Ure, and Desy Simmons
- **Email marketing for Dummies** by Arnold

. . .

Get a Face Lift.

Update your eBay store.

I'm a meat and potatoes kind of guy. I like my food dull and bland, but sometimes you gotta put on a little glitz. A lot of eBay sellers have revitalized their business by giving their listings a facelift.

Pay attention when you are shopping or researching items on eBay. Fancy listing pages and glitzy store fronts catch your eye. Done properly, they instill confidence in the seller and make you think they are successful and trustworthy.

You can find web designers on eBay, Elance, and Fiverr to help you with this project. Prices can run from as little as five dollars to as much as five or ten thousand dollars, but the payoffs can be huge if you find the right design.

Start slow if you need to.

Have a custom logo and listing header designed for your eBay store. As time goes on, add a custom listing template, and then a fancy store front.

If you can't afford the expense right now use eBay's store design tools to add a search bar to your store header. Set-up custom categories and subcategories for your eBay store. This makes it easier for shoppers to locate items within your store. Add a couple of promotion boxes to your storefront. Use one to collect email addresses, and another to promote sale items, or shipping specials.

As soon as you are able, put a plan together so you can build a great looking eBay store.

. . .

Check out eBay's app store.

eBay has some great apps available to make running your business smoother. Take a few moments every now and then to page through them. Maybe even try a few of them out.

Here are a few apps I recommend.

- **GoDaddy Bookkeeping** makes it easy to track sales and profits, so you know how well your business is doing at any point. GoDaddy Bookkeeping automatically imports sales and purchase information from eBay and PayPal. It lets you connect bank accounts and credit cards you use in your business. If you sell on eBay, Amazon, and other ecommerce platforms it lets you collect sales data from all of them in one spot. The cost is $9.99 a month, but it's worth it.

- **Endicia Int'l. Advisor** helps you keep track of international shipping rates and requirements. For sellers who ship internationally without using the Global Shipping Program Endicia can help you get rates right. You can also use the full version of Endicia to fulfill all your domestic and international shipping needs. Costs start at $9.99 per month.

- **Smart Social** is an app that helps you target your eBay listings to followers on Facebook and Twitter. Smart Social lets sellers send listings out one at a time or in batches of 25. You can also set up smart rules to govern how your listings are shared. It's a free app so give it a whirl and see how social media can help grow your sales.

- **My Store Maps** displays locations you have previously shipped packages to. The concept sounds a little cheesy, but many sellers swear by it. Using the app is free.

- **WWW Domain 4 My Store** lets sellers set up a custom domain for your eBay store. Sellers can do it themselves, but it takes some technical know how about domain forwarding to get it right. When you use this app all the heavy lifting is done for you.

Workshop 1
Craft an Amazing Title

Everyone who buys something from you is going to read your title. Everyone who does and doesn't buy from you is going to read your title. Make it compelling, and buyers will click on your listing. Make it so so, and they will move on to the next item.

Here's something else you need to know. Over fifty percent of the people who buy from you only look at the title and pictures in your listing. They won't read your description, your policies, or anything else. If the title and pictures look good, they will click buy—even if they are not sure about what they are buying.

That could mean trouble down the line.

But, for now, let's concentrate on how to create a clickable title. A title that answers all your buyer's questions and makes them want to learn more.

As I said earlier, your title doesn't need to be a literary masterpiece. It doesn't even have to make sense. Its sole purpose is to grab a potential buyer's attention and get them to click on your listing.

eBay gives you eighty characters to describe your item. Your goal is to cram every detail and keyword you can into those eighty characters.

The first thing to know is your title is how people are going to find the item you are selling on eBay. eBay uses the words in your title to determine who will see your article. Because of this, it is important to use every possible word or combination of words someone might search by in the title.

Your title doesn't have to read well or even make sense to be effective. It just needs to contain as many keywords as possible to maximize the chances it will be displayed when someone searches for a similar item.

Unfortunately, many people waste this valuable space trying to get cutesy or to write a sentence that makes sense. The fact is no one is going to search for, "very nice," "awesome," "great," or "one-of-a-kind." You would be much better off giving a professional descriptor like "near-mint" or "MS65," because these are terms collectors are looking for.

Here are some tips to write better titles:

- **Include as many keywords as possible**. You've got eighty characters. Use as many of them as you can in each of your titles. Don't worry that your title doesn't make sense. Just be sure to include all the keywords you think someone would use to describe the item you are selling.

- **Double Check Your Spelling**. To increase your chances of getting discovered, spell everything correctly. If you are in doubt, use spell check.
- **Avoid using adjectives and descriptive phrases**. Save all the adjectives and descriptive phrases for your item description. No one searches for "very nice" – "LQQK" – or "WoW!"
- **Avoid excess capitalization**. No one likes it when you shout or try too hard to sell them. If you absolutely must use all capitalization, only do it to one word, not your entire title.
- **Use the correct terms**. If you are totally unfamiliar with the item you are selling, Google it. One thing I've discovered over the years is people love to email you and criticize you when you spell a word incorrectly, put an item in the wrong category, or describe it wrong. Sometimes it feels like they are crawling out of the woodwork and gunning for you.
- **Include common misspellings**. If the item you are selling is frequently misspelled on eBay,

include the misspellings in your title if you have room.

- **Don't use abbreviations**. Abbreviations confuse customers. If there is any doubt, spell it out. If you don't have room in your title for the word you want to use, chose another word with a similar meaning. The exception here would be commonly accepted abbreviations on eBay. NWT – New with tags, NIB – New in the box, BNWT – Brand new with tags, FS – Factory sealed.

With all that said, one of the hardest things for many sellers to do is decide which keywords to put in your title.

Perhaps the easiest way to determine which keywords to include in your title is to look at other auctions for similar items. How do they describe the item? What keywords do they use? What words do you see show up in other auctions?

After you've made your list, take a minute to put yourself in the buyer's shoes. What words would you use to describe the item you are selling? Those are the keywords you want to include in your title.

Workshop 2
Craft an Amazing Description

It never ceases to amaze me when I see a high-end listing with a one-line description.

WTF!

Other than your title and pictures, your description is the best tool you have to nail it and close the sale. Don't get lazy now! Ask yourself, what is it going to take to move someone from maybe—to, "Hell Yeah!"

Here's what I mean.

The following description accompanied a book currently listed for sale on eBay with an asking price of $349.99. It reads:

Samuel Brown. An Authentic History of the Second War for Independence. (Auburn, 1815) vol.1. 6 5/8 inch high.

Not much to go on is there?

The seller posted six high-resolution photos that give you a good idea of the condition. From what I can see, the cover is in good shape with some minor chipping. I don't see much foxing or yellowing on the pages, but I can only see four of them, so I can't be sure. And, what about the binding? Is it tight? Are the pages about ready to bust loose from the seams? And, does anyone know? Is it a first or second edition?

Face it. There are a lot of unanswered questions here.

I love old books, especially from the period covering the Revolutionary War to the Civil War, but I would have to pass on this one. I can't help asking myself, what issues is the seller hiding from me?

It's a shame really, because it's an important early work on the War of 1812, and the price is right on the money.

The seller could have turned the whole thing around if he'd taken time out to ask himself, what information does the buyer need to make an informed decision? Does he (or she) need to know more about the condition? The content? Or, what sellers on other sites are charging for that book?

As soon as you answer those questions, you can craft an amazing description that tells potential buyers everything they need to know to move from maybe to yes.

Try this one on for size:

> *Samuel Brown. An Authentic History of the Second War for Independence. (Auburn, 1815) vol.1.*
>
> *If you are interested in the War of 1812, the book is a must have. Brown served as a private in the Ohio Militia. He fought against the Shawnee Chief Tecumseh at the Battle of Thames and pursued the British troops after the Battle of Lake Erie.*
>
> *The book itself is in excellent condition. It's volume one of a two-part series and would make an excellent addition to any Military Collection. The only other copy listed online is available from Biblio for $850 (for both volumes).*
>
> *The book is 6 ½ inches tall by 4 ½ inches wide. There are some mild foxing and age spots, but everything is readable. There's a faded name, penciled on the flyleaf, and some scattered pencil marks on the first few pages (see scans). From the research I've done, it's not the first edition, but it is an 1815 printing.*

Do you see the difference?

This description answers the questions buyers need to know to make an informed decision. It tells you the title, publication, size, page condition, and provides a brief biography of the author. It lets you know, it's rare. There's only one other copy available online, and it's selling for a hefty premium.

Could we have made it even better?

Sure. If it had been one of my listings, I would have shared several excerpts of battles and troop movements. At the very least, I would have linked to a PDF copy online at *Google Books* or the *Library of Congress*. A lot of sellers are afraid to do that because they think a buyer will read the free copy and take a pass on the listing. Not so. Collectors want to make sure of what they are buying. The best way to do that is to let them preview the content. Serious collectors will give the content a quick read through to validate it fits in with their collection. Window-shoppers will read the free content and move on to the next listing. Good riddance to them. We want buyers, not lookers.

Here's another example:

Original Niles Weekly Register published on August 6, 1814.

This issue contains a lengthy detailed article about the Battle of Chippewa on the Niagara Frontier.

Excerpt:

"Early on July 5, British light infantry, militia, and Indians crossed the Chippawa ahead of Riall's main body and began sniping at Scott's outposts from the woods to their west. (Some of them nearly captured Scott, who was having breakfast in a farmhouse.) Brown ordered Porter's brigade and Indians to clear the woods. They did so, but they met Riall's advancing regulars and hastily retreated.

"Scott was already advancing from Street's Creek. His artillery (Captain Nathaniel Towson's company, with three 12-pounder guns) deployed on the portage road and opened fire. Riall's own guns (two light 24-pounder guns and a 5.5-inch howitzer) attempted to reply, but Towson's guns destroyed an ammunition wagon and put most of the British guns out of action.

"As the redcoats of the 1st and 100th Regiments moved forward, their own artillery had to stop firing in order to avoid hitting them. Meanwhile, the American gunners switched from firing round shot to firing canister, with lethal consequences for the British infantry. Once the opposing lines had closed to less than

100 yards apart, Scott advanced his wings, forming his brigade into a "U" shape which allowed his flanking units to catch Riall's advancing troops in a heavy crossfire.

"Both lines stood and fired repeated volleys; after 25 minutes of this pounding Riall, his own coat pierced by a bullet, ordered a withdrawal. The 1/8th, which had been moving to the right of the other two regiments, formed line to cover their retreat. As they in turn fell back, three British 6-pounder guns came into action to cover their withdrawal, with two more 6-pounders firing from the entrenchments north of the Chippawa. Scott halted his brigade, although some of Porter's Iroquois pursued the British almost to the Chippawa."

Very good condition. This listing includes the complete entire original newspaper, NOT just a clipping or a page of it. We stand behind all the items we sell with a "no questions asked, money back guarantee." Every item we sell is an original newspaper printed on the date indicated at the beginning of its description. U.S. buyers pay $8 priority mail postage which includes waterproof plastic and a heavy cardboard flat to protect your purchase from damage in the mail. Ask about International shipping rates. We do combine postage (to *reduce postage costs) for multiple purchases sent in the same package.*

What do you think?

It answers all the questions a buyer could have. It describes the item, provides several excerpts focused on the information collectors want, need, and are willing to pay for. And, it offers buyers a 100% Money Back Guarantee.

I know. It's a lot of work.

It takes some extra time to write a description like this, but when you do, you are more likely to command a premium price.

It's up to you.

You can do what every other seller does, and post a half-assed description, or you can put in the time it takes to craft a detailed item description guaranteed to sell your item.

I know it works.

I did it for sixteen years and built a strong business with thousands of repeat buyers.

If you want to sell on eBay or any other e-commerce website, this is the type of listing page you need to craft.

Workshop 3
The Price is Right

Pricing is the toughest part of selling online. It's where the rubber meets the road. It's where everything comes together

A lot of sellers start every listing at 99 cents. Others stick an outlandish price on every item they list, then slap on a buy it now. Both approaches work. Neither is a viable strategy for building a long-term business.

Pricing is one of the trickiest parts of selling on eBay or any online site, for that matter.

Price your item too high, and no one will buy it. Price your item too low, and you will be leaving profit on the table. The problem is there is no one hundred percent perfect method for pricing your item right out of the box. Pricing is more of a process, especially if you are selling multiple copies of an item.

For some items, pricing is easy. Commodity items people buy every day like foodstuffs, DVD's, books, electronics, all sell in a very close price range. If you step out of the accepted price range for the item, your sales will dry up quicker than you think.

Perhaps the easiest way to price your item is to search eBay to see what similar items have recently sold for. To do this, you need to use the advanced search function.

To access the Advanced Search feature, go to the top of the eBay page. To the right of the search box, you will see the word **Advanced** just after the big blue Search box. Go ahead and click on the word **Advanced**.

Type in the name or description of the item you want to search for. Scroll down a little further where it says search including and check the box by **Completed Listings**. Then click enter. It returns a list of all the ended listing for that item within the past thirty days. Items listed in green are items that have sold.

After you've done this, you will be able to see a list of all completed items on eBay. The unsold listing will appear for thirty days; sold listings will appear for ninety days. After it returns this list, you have the option to narrow your search down even further by clicking on active listings (with bids) or completed listings.

The great thing here is you can see how much items like yours have recently sold for on eBay.

By looking through completed listings, you can easily find the price range your item has sold in. There's no need to guess about how to price your items.

The way I use the information is to look through the titles to find items most like mine. Each time I click on an item, I take a few notes about any keywords the seller used in the title and item description. I also make a note of the price it sold for. If it was an auction item, I mark down the starting price. Next, I look at shipping to determine if the seller offered free shipping or the options and prices they offered for shipping.

After you do this for four or five items, you will have some great information about how to write your item description and title. It should give you an excellent idea of what you can expect your item to sell for.

At this point, we're almost ready to start pricing your item. Before you stop doing your research, I'd suggest you also click into two or three of the items that sold for the highest prices. Look over the notes you made and see if these listings said anything different than the other ones you looked at. Specifically, did they offer a more detailed description? Did they use different keywords in the title? Did they start at a lower price? Did they use a buy-it-now?

Now you need to determine a pricing strategy.

Some people swear by starting everything at 99 cents or $9.99 and letting the market determine the price. The problem with this strategy is it only works for certain categories of items. If you are selling something that always closes in a tight price range like electronics, cell phones, iPhones, iPads, and the like, starting your item at 99 cents is going to bring in the maximum number of bidders, and will usually bring you the highest price possible for each item.

If you sell one of a kind items, collectibles, and other low demand items, starting your item at 99 cents is going to be a disaster. What's going to happen in nine out of ten cases is, if your item sells at all, it's going to sell for 99 cents, or $1.04.

A better pricing strategy with many items is to price them at the lowest price you are willing to accept and then add a buy-it-now at what you would like to get. If you are selling your item in a fixed price format, set the price somewhat higher than you hope to get, and add best offer to it.

What if you are selling something unique, that isn't currently available on eBay? How do you price your item then?

If it's something you have a lot of or a lot of similar items, the best thing you can do is experiment with different price points and determine which one sells the most items.

Let me give you an example. I sell old magazine articles, removed from bound publications. So basically, all I'm selling is a few sheets of old paper. I have a few competitors on eBay, but not many.

When I first started selling magazine articles back in 2000, I priced all my items at $12.99, and they sold well. After six months I increased my price to $15.99, then $19.99, and then $25.99, and sales increased each time. When I stretched it again to $27.99, sales started slowing down. As a result, I knew my optimal price range was somewhere between $19.99 and $25.99.

I found my sweet spot in auction pricing the same way. I started my items at $9.99, and many of them sold. Then I added Buy-it-Now at 15.99, $19.99, and $25.99. Once again $25.99 provided the most conversions, so that's the formula I went with – a $9.99 starting price, with a $25.99 Buy-it-Now.

It was a great price strategy, and it worked for years.

The next thing you know, eBay decided they wanted to be more like Amazon, and to become more of a marketplace so they could lure in the big sellers like Best Buy and Toy-R-Us.

One of the things they did was to change the emphasis to fixed price listings rather than auctions. That sent me back to the drawing board, and once again, I reinvented my eBay business, this time focusing it on fixed price listings, with a just a scattering of auction listings.

Workshop 4
Make it Mobile Friendly

During the 2017 Holiday Season over half of the purchases made on eBay occurred on mobile devices. But, here's the funny thing. Most people didn't pay for their purchases on a mobile device. They saved the item to their cart, then moved to a laptop or desktop to make their payment.

It doesn't make sense, does it?

Unless. Maybe shoppers need to take a breather to make sure they are making the right decision? Or, perhaps they want to take one last look at what their purchase looks like on the big screen? Or, could it be shoppers are afraid to share their payment information on a mobile device?

Whatever the reason, the implications are clear.

You are not going to close every sale on the first click. Instead, many sales are going to be a two-part process. The risk is shoppers are going to abandon items in their carts.

e-Tailers are going to need to deploy enhanced reminder systems, to counteract this trend.

At Christmas time, I searched out Iowa Hawkeye hoodies on eBay. Like many other shoppers, I added two of them to my cart but never got around to completing the purchase. Two months later, eBay is still emailing me constant reminders—return to eBay to complete your purchase—finish your transaction now and save ten percent (get FREE shipping or whatever today's current win back offer is).

Some shoppers tuck items into their carts just to see what offers they will receive to complete the sale. On eBay, this strategy won't pay off because eBay doesn't control pricing—individual sellers do. But, on Amazon, it's a different story. Amazon is the seller of many of their items. If they want to make a deal and move some product, they are free to wheel and deal.

. . .

The growth of mobile shopping is no surprise. eBay, Amazon, Shopify and other websites have been counting down to the fifty percent mark for years. Now that we've reached that benchmark, mobile sales are only going to go up. The challenge for sellers is how to optimize their listing to provide shoppers with the best possible mobile experience.

One way, eBay is preparing for the uptick in mobile shopping is the elimination of all active content in listings by June of 2017. Included in the ban are Javascript, Flash plug-ins, and form actions. eBay says the use of these features can, "negatively impact the user experience by inhibiting mobile purchasing, increasing page load times, and increasing security vulnerabilities."[a]

They also recommend sellers stop investing in custom store design "since this capability will [be] retired at a later date."

Eliminating custom store design is huge because it's what has distinguished eBay from Amazon. Many sellers have developed their businesses into multi-million dollar enterprises by branding their stores. After this capability goes away growing your business is going to be much harder. It's going to make it harder for one seller to distinguish themselves from another, but it also gives us a significant clue as to what direction eBay is going.

Think commodity selling, the same as on Amazon, with one listing page and many sellers tagging along.

The switch to mobile and away from active content is good and bad. Good in that eBay is chasing market trends so that they can keep up with changing

[a] http://pages.ebay.com/sell/itemdescription/bestpractices.html

technologies; bad in that it marks the beginning of a new trend in eBay selling.

Make no mistake about it, there is going to be a shakeup for eBay sellers in the not-to-distant future. Examine your options now. Determine how it is going to impact your eBay business, and take appropriate actions.

. . .

Getting back to mobile.

eBay created a mobile friendly checker so that you can see how your items will display on portable devices. Check it our here.

http://www.ebay.com/tools/sell/mobile-friendly-test

Tips to make your listings mobile friendly

- eBay also suggests you should add the following HTML code to your listings. <meta name="viewport" content="width=device-width, initial-scale=1">. It tells the mobile browser how to "adjust the dimensions and scaling" so they display properly on mobile devices.
- If you run thousands of listings on eBay, you should act now and ensure your listing are compliant with the new mobile friendly policies before eBay starts taking them down.

- If you have a custom listing template, consider eliminating it, or contact your listing designer so they can create one that complies with the new policies.

- Consider writing shorter item descriptions. eBay announced they would pull a 250-character description from your listing to display in mobile searches. But, they did announce a way to display more text on mobile—write shorter listings, under 800 characters. If you do that, they will show your entire description.

Workbook 5
eBay Global Shipping Program

(Most of this section was first published in my book eBay Shipping Simplified: How to Store, Package, and Ship the Items You Sell on eBay, Amazon, and Etsy. For most eBayers, the transition to International shipping is scary at first—but it doesn't have to be. This section introduces you to the eBay Global Shipping Program—it's a pain-free way to get started selling internationally.)

Several years ago, eBay introduced their Global Shipping Program. It's an easy way for sellers to jump into international selling without having to worry about shipping rules, customs forms, etc.

If you've been itching to get started with international sales but were afraid of the extra work involved I suggest that you give it a shot using eBay's Global Shipping Program.

Many small sellers are terrified of international shipping. They've heard so many horror stories they are scared to give it a shot. They don't want to fill out customs forms or worry about whether their package is going to make it all the way to Timbuktu or not.

eBay has eliminated all that grief for sellers who use their Global Shipping Program. Sellers list their items just like they normally would. When the item sells you ship it to an eBay shipping center in the United States.

Bing Badda Boom! As soon as it arrives at the shipping center, your responsibility for the shipment is over. From that point on eBay and their shipping partners assume any liability for getting your package to its destination.

Here's how it works.

When you list your item for sale on eBay check the box to include your item in the Global Shipping Program and you are good to go.

Some categories don't qualify for inclusion in the Global Shipping Program. When you bump into these, eBay will flag the item and let you know. I do a lot of selling in the collectible category. Collectibles made before 1899 don't qualify, so I see this issue pop up quite often. The only way around it is to ship the item internationally yourself. I'll discuss this option in more detail later.

When an item sells using the Global Shipping Program sellers can't send the buyer an invoice. eBay takes care of all this for you. The reason is you have no way of knowing what their shipping fee will be.

Once the customer pays, you will receive a payment notification along with the shipping address for your package. The easiest way to recognize a payment made through the Global Shipping Program is the address will include a long reference number.

Ship your item like you normally would. Include delivery confirmation, so you can ensure the shipping center received your item. Once you have confirmation the item was received, your part in the transaction is complete.

eBay's shipping partner—Pitney Bowes—will readdress your package, fill out all the appropriate customs forms, and ensure delivery to the customer.

Overall the Global Shipping Program is an excellent way to increase your sales. During my peak selling period, international sales accounted for roughly thirty-five to forty percent of my eBay sales and profits.

If you are looking for an easy fix to grow your sales, opt into the Global Shipping Program and give it a shot.

Bonus 1 – Do These Things First

From my experience, there are certain things sellers can do that will make them more successful.

If you are a seller teetering on the brink of success instituting some of these changes could give you the extra nudge you've been looking for to break into the big time. If you are a new seller, there's no better time to get started doing things the right way. You don't have any bad habits to break. Just jump in and get started.

Keep in mind—this is stuff that has worked for me with the items I sell. Not everything will work for you. Keep doing what works for you—adjust or discard the rest.

Remove all HTML code from your listings.

eBay Search does not play well with HTML code—especially when you have HTML code in the listing header.

I love a fancy listing template that has a great design and perfectly formatted pictures, but what I like even better is listening to the cash register ding on my eBay app.

If your sales are down, and nothing you do is working—strip the header out of a few listings, remove all that fancy formatting and templates out of a few more. Then see what happens.

If unformatted listings allow you to make more sales, that's the way to go. By doing this, you can decide for yourself what works and what doesn't.

After you post a listing, view it on your tablet and smartphone. If you have trouble viewing your listing re-work it or cancel the listing and start over.

The internet today is all about mobile.

People constantly check their phones, tablets, and Kindles all day long for new emails, tweets, and Facebook updates. Last Christmas, nearly fifty percent of holiday shopping, took place on mobile devices. This year that number is expected to be closer to sixty percent.

If your listing isn't optimized for mobile, you are going to miss out on over fifty percent of the customers searching for your items.

At the end of the day when you finish listing items, check some of them on your smartphone or iPad. Ensure that your items appear in search and are optimized for mobile viewing. If you inserted your photos into your listing using HTML code or a listing application like Auctiva or Ink Frog your pictures are going to appear small and they will be hard to view. If you posted them using eBay's list your item page, your pictures would expand to fill the entire device screen, and potential buyers will be able to use the arrow keys to move between one picture and another.

Ask yourself which format you are more likely to buy from and make the appropriate changes.

Get straight to the point.

Less is better. People are in a hurry to get things done. The easier you make it to buy from you, the more stuff you are going to sell.

People are lazy.

They read auction descriptions the same way they read blog posts and everything else on the internet. They scan the description for words that catch their fancy.

They cruise through bullet points for a quick overview. They glance at the captions for pictures.

If they run into a big blob of text, they are going to click the back-arrow button and move on to the next listing. White space, bullet points, and bold headings are your allies in making more sales.

Include more and better pictures.

A good fifty percent of buyers make their decision just by looking at the pictures in your listing. They don't have time to read, or they don't want to read your item description. Many foreign buyers can't read or understand your description. They rely solely on the pictures you include to make their decision.

Some sellers play to this.

They include lots of close-up pictures and encourage buyers to check the pictures and decide for themselves if the item meets their needs.

Focus on the 80 /20 rule.

Concentrate on selling the 20% of articles that bring you the most profit. Scrap the slow sellers.

If you are like most sellers, a few of your items account for most of your sales volume.

If you have an eBay store the odds are you have hundreds, maybe thousands of items languishing in there. Maybe ten or twenty sell every month, but the rest of them just sit there—festering. They suck up your monthly free listings and cost you additional listing fees. They taunt you into working extra hours hoping they'll be that one other sale you need to buy a new iPhone or an extra appetizer at lunch.

Quit playing the longshots.

Take aim and start focusing on sure things. Concentrate on the twenty percent of items that sell the best. Don't waste time and money on listings that rarely sell.

Don't try to reinvent the wheel.

It's great to find a new product that no one else has and will sell like hotcakes. There are very few items like that. If you focus all your time on looking for the newest greatest thing, you are going to miss out on a lot of sure things.

Everyone wishes they could go back in time and be the first guy in on the Hula Hoop craze, the Pet Rock, or the Chia Pet, but—those kinds of things are a one in a million shot. If you concentrate all your effort on the long ball, you are going to miss the sure hits along the way.

Sure, catching the wave on a new fad can make you wealthy and famous, but selling sure things like denim jackets, vintage toys, etc. will keep the cash registers ringing day in and day out. The will put food on the table, and gas in your tank.

Chasing fads will suck up listing fees, the time you could spend posting profitable items, and free time you could have invested with your family and friends.

Don't beat a dead horse.

Things run out of gas. They stop selling for one reason or another. Know when to call it quits and move on to a new niche.

Good things come to an end.

I've spent the last fifteen years selling vintage magazine articles, prints, and advertisements. Sales have been slugging along in low gear since the recession of 2008. eBay's move to fixed price listings is another nail in their coffin. Sales are down, selling prices are down, and profits are down.

I'm beating a dead horse.

I have two choices—reinvent myself or reimagine my product line. It's hard. We've been together for fifteen years. There's still money coming in—sometimes thousands of dollars a month, but it's nothing like it was.

The challenge for 2019 is to reinvent my business and carve out a new niche.

What about you? If you are beating a dead horse, do you have the plan to put it down, or breathe new life into it?

Spend more time following up with customers.

Chit chat. Shoot the shit. It's going to help you build a relationship with customers and sell more stuff.

Getting to know your customers doesn't need to take that long. You just need to make it a regular part of your business day. When someone asks about an item you have for sale—answer their question. Take a few minutes to thank them for contacting you. Talk up your item, and your product line. Ask how they are going to use it, and what other things they would like to see you offer.

If it's close to a holiday—wish them a "Merry Christmas!" or a "Happy Easter!" If you want to be politically correct, wish them a "happy holiday season." Getting to know your customers only takes a few moments, but it gives buyers a warm and fuzzy feeling about doing business with you.

Try new things.

Complacency has killed more businesses than anything else. Try to sell at least one new product every week. At the end of the year, if only five of them take off you will still have a stronger product line.

Products and entire product lines go stale. Things become obsolete. People become obsolete if they don't change. Think back to the guys you knew in high school and college. How many of them are still reliving their glory days? It's great to spend five or ten minutes with them and reminisce, but then you start to get this queasy feeling—this guy's not going anywhere. He's stuck in the past.

Products are the same as people. They get stuck in a certain period.

If you are not selling nostalgia, you need to cut the strings and try new things. It will make your product line stronger and force you to become a better seller.

Approach buyer protection cases rationally.

When a buyer protection case is filed against you, put aside any personal feelings, or any thoughts the customer is trying to put one over on you. Pull the trigger and give them a full refund—especially with low dollar amount items. You will feel better, and it will make you look better with your customers and with eBay.

Think of it this way.

In the larger scheme of things—what's twenty, fifty, even a hundred dollars compared to everything you sell on eBay? You may be in the right. The customer may be taking advantage you, but—is it worth lowering your ranking in search, or having your selling privileges restricted or revoked?

Probably not.

Look at the big picture and do what's right for your business. Don't let personal feelings knock you down.

Take some extra time off—just for the heck of it.

Selling on eBay is demanding. Customers are after you 24 / 7. You're rushing to list new items, and to ship old ones before your 24-hour deadline expires. Take a break now and then to make time for yourself.

Selling on eBay is tough. It never stops. There's always one more item to list, one more package to mail, and one more email to answer.

It'll tear the hell out of you if you let it and make you old before your time.

Be sure to schedule some time for yourself before you become the ogre in your basement dungeon.

Sell for charity.

eBay Giving Works makes it easy to sell for charity. Pick a national charity like the Red Cross or choose a local charity that's close to your heart.

Add two or three charity auctions to your repertoire every month. It will make you feel better about selling on eBay. It will make your customers feel better about buying from you, and it will make you more money.

Not every charity Giving Works listing sells or sells for a higher price, but they do get a lot of page views. My listings receive twenty to twenty-five-page views. When I add a charity to the listing, it draws several hundred-page views, especially when I list using a large national charity.

Even when the item doesn't sell, that's a lot of extra eyes on my listings. Many of those visitor's peek through my eBay store; some of them are likely to pick up an item or two as they're cruising through.

If you haven't tried it yet, list a couple of your items with eBay Giving Works. It just might become a habit.

Bonus # 2 - Sell it on Fiverr

(Sometimes eBay and Amazon aren't the right fit for your talents. A lot of people in my circle like to write or draw. Others are a whiz at using Photoshop. Instead of selling physical products on Amazon or eBay, they would rather sell creative services. That's where Fiverr comes in. This is an excerpt from my book <u>Fiverr Boot Camp: Join the Gig Economy. Make More Money, Enjoy More Freedom</u>.)

Fiverr is a freelance hub where buyers and sellers can exchange cash for services. What amazes me is every item featured on Fiverr starts at only $5.00—almost.

There appears to be no limit to the types of services sellers can offer on Fiverr. Among the recent gigs (what Fiverr calls listings) are –

- Custom logo design

- Facebook header design
- Amazon book reviews and product reviews
- Puppet videos
- Kindle and eBook book covers
- Tarot readings
- Psychic readings
- Resume and cover letter writing
- Poetry Writing
- Business card design
- Infographic design

By now hopefully, you get the idea. If you can imagine it, you can find a way to offer it as a gig on Fiverr.

Gig Extras -Moving Beyond $5.00

Earlier I mentioned gig extras.

Gig extras are the method Fiverr has devised to let sellers take their income to the next level. To better understand how gig extras work, check out these extras offered by Professor Puppet.

Get more with my Gig Extras

- I will post your video on YouTube so you don't have to OR Deliver your video in 1080p HD PLEASE SPECIFY +$10
  Requires no additional time

- I will superimpose your URL or any message over your video Limit 2 supers per upgrade +$10
  Requires no additional time

- I will Shoot your video on my Green Screen and superimpose a different background +$50
  Requires no additional time

- I will RUSH SERVICE, I will drop everything and make your video FIRST before anything else in the queue +$20
  Requires no additional time

Even though every gig on Fiverr starts at $5.00, Professor Puppet can increase his take to $95.00 if someone decides to add all his gig extras to their order.

And, just in case you think most buyers stick with the basic $5.00 offer, think again! Professor Puppet made two promotional videos for my businesses. Each time I spent over $35.00.

So, if anyone out there is still wondering how you can make money selling each of your services for only five bucks, you know the answer – **GIG EXTRAS**. They can quickly raise your average $5.00 sale to $25.00, or more.

One final thought on gig extras. The best gig extras don't necessarily have to cost you more time or money. Most sellers offer very simple gig extras:

- Next day service for five or ten dollars.
- A PSD file of the graphic they already designed for an additional $5.00 to $20.00. It's no extra work. You already have it on your computer.
- Two more revisions for $5.00, or $10.00.
- Your video delivered in additional formats for $10.00, or $20.00.
- A 3D cover to go with the 2D eBook cover they already designed for an additional $5.00.

The key to making the most money on Fiverr is to keep your gig extras simple and easy to perform, but still, make them appear valuable to your customers.

Tomasso has been selling on Fiverr for two years now. "I didn't worry about gig extras when I got started," he said. "I was making $2500 a month, five bucks at a time.

"Why complicate things?

"That's what I thought. But, one day I read a story on the Fiverr blog about a guy who doubled his income after he added gig extras to his listings.

"That got my attention.

"He said one out of eight orders gave him an extra ten dollars just for providing next day delivery. It didn't take any more work. He just switched up their place in the queue. He received an extra $25.00 when he charged a commercial use fee for his drawings. Again, it didn't involve any more work. He just emailed the buyer a commercial use release. Now Fiverr offers this as a gig extra, so it's even easier.

"It didn't make any sense to me, but I gave it a shot. And, crazy as it sounds, people started paying me more money.

"All I can say is try it; you'll like it."

I saved the best part for last. After sellers have asked for and collected payment for their gig extras, many sellers dangle a new-fangled cyber tip jar out there that lets them earn even more money.

If you want to make even more money, the key is to give customers a compelling, or downright crazy reason to give you an extra-large tip.

One seller suggests for an additional $5.00; he could start his day with a latte from Starbucks, for $20.00 he could put a half a tank of gas in his old jalopy, and for $50.00 he would have a good start at taking his wife out for a romantic supper.

Who could resist giving this creative genius a tip?

How do you get started?

Getting started as a seller on Fiverr is as easy as entering your email address and choosing a username and password. That's it, and you are a member of the Fiverr community.

Before you click the join button, you need to take a few moments to think about your username. It's how people will come to know you on Fiverr.

A relevant username that complements the service you are providing will help to position you as an expert in the service you are offering.

Many people choose the first idea that pops into their head, or maybe their name. The thing is, if you name your business marysue or wonderwoman 113, people aren't going to have any idea what you do.

If you call yourself videoreviewer or bestlogodesigner, people are going to know right away what services you offer. A professional username can help position you as the best seller for the job.

Seller Basics

Every gig on Fiverr starts with the words "I will ___for $5.00." Or, I should say, every gig used to say what they would do for $5.00. Now that Fiverr lets sellers set a higher starting price it says, "I will_____." The title no longer contains a price.

As a seller, your job is to fill in the blank. Just what is it you are willing to do for five bucks?

I know, some of you are saying—not much.

A recent Fiverr survey says there are thousands of sellers making $1000 to $2000, or more, every month. Some of the elite Fiverrs make $5000 or more each, and every month.

So, before you turn your nose up at five bucks, let's examine some of the things you need to consider before creating your first gig.

Before you do anything, check out the Fiverr website for two or three days. Explore the different categories and click into as many gigs as you can.

Keep your pen and notebook handy. Whenever you see something you like or a gig you might want to do – jot it down.

Write down the seller's username—the title of their gig—keywords they use to describe their gig—any special instructions they include in their descriptions. It's valuable information you can use later to help craft your gigs.

Don't stop there.

Check out any pictures, or samples they include. If the seller has a video describing the service they are offering, watch it, and make a few notes about what they say, and how they describe their gig.

Read the feedback left for some of the gigs that tickle your fancy. What did buyers like, or dislike, about them? What they say can give you clues to help you design a better gig, and position it, so more people will choose to do business with you.

You don't have to pick out your first gig right now, just jot down as many ideas as you can.

Study your list of possible gigs.

Draw a star by the ones you think would be a good fit for you. Cross off the ones you don't think would be a good fit for you, or you can't see yourself doing.

Okay. This is where the rubber meets the road. At this point, you should have at least five gigs you think would give you a great start on Fiverr.

Make sure the gigs you choose are something you can make money doing.

Most sellers agree to earn money you need to offer a service you can complete in no more than fifteen minutes. Five minutes or less is even better.

At fifteen minutes per gig, and an average profit of $4.00 per gig, that means you can make $16.00 per hour. If you can lower your working time to ten minutes per gig, you can make $24.00 per hour.

Now go back and evaluate the gig ideas you picked out. Be brutally honest.

Is this something you can do in fifteen minutes, or less? If not, is there a way you can do it faster? If not, scratch this gig off your list, or move it to your "needs work" pile.

Continue to evaluate each potential gig the same way.

If you are sure, you can complete them in fifteen minutes or less, great! Add them to your list of must do gigs.

The last step is to work a couple of your potential gigs to make sure how fast you can do them. Use a stopwatch to track your time. Make a list of your gigs by how much time they took you to complete.

"Don't skip this step," cautions Jon. "Every time I pass on testing, it comes back to bite me. Anymore, If I can't finish a gig in five to eight minutes, I say the hell with it.

"My goal is forty bucks an hour. If a gig doesn't let me make that, I shelve it, no matter how many sales I think I can make."

Pick the gig you want to get started on today.

From here on out we're going to concentrate on getting this gig ready to post on Fiverr.

Create Your First Gig

Posting a gig on Fiverr consists of nine simple steps.

For this demonstration, we are going to assume you are going to sell a Kindle book cover. As we walk through the steps, take some time to reflect on each step, and how the process relates to creating your gig.

One of my favorite book cover designers created the gig we're going to examine next. Right now, she has 86 orders in her queue, so you know this lady is breaking her ass to get them done. But at the same time, she's making some serious bucks.

To get started, choose the Start Selling button at the top of Fiverr's main page.

Step 1. The first thing you are going to see are the familiar words, "I will _____ for $5.00." Now that gigs can start at more than five dollars it's no longer part of the form. You can still state the dollar amount if it gives you a one up on your competition.

Tell people what you are willing to do for $5.00. A good gig title should be short, tell people exactly what you are going to do for them, and be rich in keywords.

Look at the title of this gig. "I will design a professional and unique eBook cover or Kindle cover for $5.00."

It's a great title. It contains three main keywords "design," "eBook cover," and "Kindle cover." It also has two descriptors or adjectives "professional" and "unique."

The right keywords will give it an excellent shot at being picked up and shown by Fiverr's search engine every time someone searches for either "eBook cover" or "Kindle cover."

Step 2. Select a category. The beautiful thing here is Fiverr makes choosing a category super-easy. They only give you twelve choices: Fun & Bizarre, Online Marketing, Graphics and Design, Advertising, Writing & Translation, Lifestyle, Business, Programming & Tech, Other, Music & Audio, Gifts, and Video and Animation.

Pick the category that best describes your gig. It will give you the best bang for your buck.

Step 3. Description. Tell your story. Tell people what you are selling, what the benefits are for them, and what information you need from them to make it happen. If there are things you cannot, or will not do, this is the place to say it. A lot of sellers that offer art and writing services specify they won't write or draw pornography.

Remember, it's your business. What you choose to do, or not do, is up to you.

Let's look at the description in our sample listing.

"Over 5,000 covers created to date! 3D Covers are FREE, and when I say three days, I mean three days – regardless of the orders in the queue...and I'm not happy until you are so--UNLIMITED REVISIONS! Order now! * I also create covers for ALL genres, so let's hear what you have in mind. What makes my covers stand out from other designers here on Fiverr? I treat your cover as an individual! Are cars the theme of your book? How do metallic fonts and backgrounds sound? Chocolate the theme? We'll make book buyers want to lick the cover itself! Trust me; you'll love your cover. Order now!"

What do you think?

This description offers so many examples of the things you should try to include for every one of your gigs. The seller tells you twice to "Order Now!" She tells you once in the middle, and again at the end.

She emphasizes her covers are different from those made by other designers on Fiverr. Then she tells you what makes them better and different – "We'll make book buyers want to lick the cover itself!"

She guarantees people who purchase her gig they will be pleased with their cover. "I'm not happy until you are so—UNLIMITED REVISIONS!"

Take some time to read through the descriptions written by many different Top-Rated-Sellers, and you will quickly learn the secrets to being more successful and selling more gigs on Fiverr.

Step 4. Instructions to Buyer. Tell viewers what information you need to put their order together.

Fiverr uses this box to request information to help you complete the order, so before you fill it out, take a few minutes to carefully decide what information you need to make the project come together. The clearer you are with your instructions, the easier it will be to complete your project in as little time as possible.

Another benefit will be better feedback because you delivered your gig on time, and exactly how the buyer wanted it.

Step 5. Tags. Tags are simply a list of keywords people use to search for your gig on Fiverr.

ebook cover books design web kindle dsn

A simple way to pick your tags is to see what keywords other sellers are using to tag their gigs. Choose the keywords you think are relevant and add them here.

Step 6. Maximum days to complete. What's the longest it will take you to deliver the finished gig? As a new seller, you should strive to complete every gig within twenty-four hours.

People like fast.

Everybody wants to buy something today and get it yesterday. Many buyers will choose your gig over someone else's when you offer one day service, especially when other sellers list a three to five-day turnaround.

Only offer one-day turnaround if you can deliver on it. You will hurt your rankings and increase your chances of receiving negative feedback if you deliver late. If you are unsure you can finish your gig in one day, determine how many days it will take you to complete your gig and then shoot to deliver it early whenever you can. That will give buyers a pleasant surprise, and happy buyers mean good reviews.

Step 7. Add image. Upload images to illustrate your gig. These should be the best samples of your work. For illustrations, Fiverr recommends a .jpeg format, 600 pixels wide x 370 pixels high, with a maximum file size of 5 megabytes. Once you have your pictures ready, you can use MS Paint or another graphics program to resize them to 600 x 370 pixels.

It is also recommended you upload a video. It can be something as simple as you saying how you produce your gigs, giving instructions on the information you need from the seller to complete their order, or a collage showing your gigs and comments from the people who purchased them.

Keep it simple. Be informative. Better yet, make it humorous.

Step 8. This item requires shipping. If you are sending a physical product to buyers such as a small craft, check this box.

Step 9. Press the **Save** button.

Before you select save, take a few minutes to look it over first.

- Did you spell everything correctly?

- Did you include enough keywords in your title and description?
- Are your tags or keywords ones that buyers will use to search for your gig?
- Did you include all the information you're going to require in your information request line?

When you're happy with everything, press **Save**, and your gig will go live.

Pretty simple, right?

Here are a few things you should keep in mind as you begin your career on Fiverr:

- Sellers can list a maximum of twenty gigs at one time. Choose the gigs you offer carefully. Make sure they are gigs you can complete the quickest, and that will sell the best.
- When you are first starting out, you are only allowed to offer two gig extras, but many sellers have found a workaround for this. They suggest buyers should purchase an additional gig if they want something extra. For example, if your gig is to write a 200-word SEO article for $5.00, you could mention that buyers "should purchase an additional gig for every extra 200 words. It gives you the same benefit as offering a gig extra.

- Be careful about the types of gigs you offer. Reviews and testimonials are big business on Fiverr, but bogus book or product reviews for Amazon items is against Amazon's terms of service. What you will discover is many of these reviewers have a very short lifespan on Fiverr, because they quickly get shut down.
- Always offer a great value for the money you are charging. It will come back to you in good reviews and more business over the long haul.
- Spend at least a half-hour every week checking through the gigs offered on Fiverr. Try to spot new trends and services you may not currently be offering. New services will help you to grow your business and keep your offerings fresh and relevant.

Fiverr Selling 101

Fiverr continues to reinvent itself, as the freelance marketplace evolves. Gigs are no longer required to start at $5.00, but most buyers offer a $5.00 gig as a gateway to more expensive offerings.

"Five dollars is the sweet spot to reel buyers in," says Martin.

"When you start at five dollars, more people look at your gig. Position it right. Create great gig extras and package attributes, and you will make the big bucks.

"All my listings start at five dollars, but my average sale is $22.00. Take that times 273 sales a month and life is good. Very good!"

We've already talked about gig extras.

Depending upon your seller level they give you an incredible opportunity to boost your income while customizing your gigs to meet buyer wants and needs.

Package attributes is a relatively new feature that can boost your sales.

If you have spent any time on Fiverr, you probably know what I'm talking about—even if you don't recognize the name.

	$5 Basic	$10 Standard	$15 Premium
Description	Basic Package	Premium Package	Pro Package
	A front cover of the book	A front cover, back cover and spine of the book	A front cover, back cover, spine and 3D image of the book
Back & Side	–	✔	✔
3D Image	–	–	✔
Delivery Time	⦿ 2 days ◯ 1 day (+$5)	⦿ 3 days ◯ 1 day (+$10)	⦿ 3 days ◯ 1 day (+$10)
	Select $5	Select $10	Select $15

What I like about package attributes is they make it easy for buyers to compare your offerings. You can offer a starter product for $5.00, a step-up for $25.00, and a bigger step-up for $50.00. Most buyers are going to pick the middle option. They don't want to go too cheap, but they don't want to blow their whole wad either.

Package attributes make it easier to convert lookers into buyers because you are offering them more choices. I don't have any definite proof, but my guess is package attributes convert better than gig extras.

Experiment with your listings and discover what works best for you.

"You are crazy if you're not using package attributes," says Jon. "It's the best way sellers have to up-sell their gig. If you are not using them, you are leaving money on the table. Lots of money."

Custom Offers are where you can make the real money. Forbes Magazine did a story about four sellers who make $15,000 a month, or more, by using custom offers. One of the ladies profiled in the article runs an executive resume writing service. She went from making $5.00 per gig to making over $300,000 last year. A lot of her business comes from creating custom resume packages and selling them for $500 to $800 each—all by sending custom offers.

Think you can't do it? Think again.

Suppose you are a graphic artist selling custom book covers. Create the listing just as you normally would. Add package attributes and gig extras to upsell regular buyers. The only thing I want you to do differently is to add an additional line at the top and bottom of your item description page. It can be as simple as, "looking for something extra-special? Contact me for a Custom Offer."

That throws it back into the buyer's court. Some of them are going to be curious and contact you. When they do, ask some discovery questions, and fire off an offer to let them know what you can do for them.

Fiverr Anywhere works hand in hand with Custom Offers to help you make larger dollar sales.

Fiverr Anywhere started out as a Google Chrome extension. Since then it was moved to the Fiverr site. To access *Fiverr Anywhere* go to the Promote Your Business section under the My Sales Tab. Click on the Generate Custom Offer tab, then create your custom offer. After you have done that, you can retrieve your link. That will let you add your offer to your website, blog, email, or social media sites.

When someone contacts you, it works just like a regular Custom Offer. Potential buyers can accept your offer or request a modification.

Use *Fiver Anywhere* and *Custom Offer* to grow your business and reach new customers off the Fiverr website.

Good-luck! And, great selling on Fiverr!

About the Author

My books offer short easy to read solutions to your e-commerce problems. You can read most of them in under an hour. The information can be used to help you sell more products on eBay and Amazon, services on Fiverr, or eBooks on Amazon and Kindle.

Selling online isn't a mystery. It doesn't even have to be difficult.

It's all about getting started. Many people I've talked with have this crazy fear of putting things up for sale on eBay and Amazon. Somehow, they get the idea they need to do this or that. They worry they don't know enough about what they're doing to do it right. They wonder what they should sell, and about whether they can even do it or not.

That's where my books come in.

They take you hand in hand and walk you through getting started selling on eBay, Amazon, Etsy, and Fiverr. They show you how to market your Kindle books.

My goal is to get you over the speed bumps so that you can be more successful from the get-go.

What are you waiting for?

Most of my books are available as audiobooks. If you prefer to listen rather than read, be sure to check them out.

Nick Vulich

Davenport, Iowa
October 15, 2018

If you enjoyed this book

Thank you for reading this book.

If you liked it or found it helpful, I'd be grateful if you would post a short review where you purchased it. Your review does help.

It helps other readers decide if this book would be a good investment for them, and it helps me to make this an even better book for you. I read all the reviews my books receive and based on what readers tell me; I can make my books even better and include the kind of information readers want and need.

Thanks again for choosing my book, and here's wishing you great sales on eBay.